Alphabet
Animals

sophie zee

Dedicated to my son,
whose fresh eyes have inspired me
to see the world anew.

alligator

bear

cow

dog

elephant

fish

gorilla

horse

iguana

jaguar

kangaroo

lion

moose

narwhale

octopus

pig

quail

rabbit

snake

turtle

urial

vulture

walrus

xenops

yak

zebra

Made in the USA
Coppell, TX
18 January 2025

44605337R00036